WANG YANI: LONGING TO PAINT

by Anne Sibley O'Brien

•

illustrated by
Xing Fei

Scott Foresman

Editorial Offices: Glenview, Illinois • New York, New York
Sales Offices: Reading, Massachusetts • Duluth, Georgia
Glenview, Illinois • Carrollton, Texas • Menlo Park, California

In central China there is a lovely area called Guilin (GWAY-lin). Guilin has many mountains. They are shaped like rows of steep haystacks. Not far away, on the Li River, is the town of Gongcheng. There, in 1975, a little girl named Yani was born.

Yani's family name was Wang. In Chinese, the family name comes first. So the little girl's full name was Wang Yani.

Wang Yani is a famous painter. She started painting at a very young age. By the time she was six years old, she had made over four thousand paintings! She became the most famous child painter in the world. This is the story of Wang Yani and how she became a painter.

Yani's father is a painter too. He and Yani are very close. When Yani was small, her father would lift her onto his shoulders. They would go for long walks. She and her father saw the sun rise over the river. They lay on their backs in fields and watched the clouds change shapes. They strolled on misty mountain paths. All this beauty impressed Yani.

As a tiny girl, Yani began to show her great imagination. She gathered stones by the river and pretended they were monkeys. She picked up pieces of pine bark. To her they were birds.

Her father kept a diary. One story tells about a time when Yani was four years old. It had been raining for days. Yani hadn't been able to go outside to play.

"Will you mail a letter for me to the sun?" she asked her father. "He'll listen to me and go where I go. He is so lazy! He waits until night to cook his meals. The sky gets black with the smoke. Then he cleans it up. So by morning it's light again."

Another time she and her father took a seven-hour boat ride. To pass the time, they began telling each other stories. They kept telling stories during the entire trip. The other passengers were amazed.

Yani grew up with painting all around her.
She often went with her father when he
traveled to paint. One day when she was two,
she was playing in her father's studio. He was
working with a few other painters. Yani picked
up some charcoal. She began to draw on the
white walls. From time to time she stood back.
She looked at what she had drawn. And she
tilted her head. She looked just like her father
when he checked his paintings. Everyone
laughed. Her father gave her a sheet of paper
to draw on instead.

From that day, Yani drew constantly. But very soon she wanted to paint. Her father had made a very special painting for the New Year. When no one was near, Yani mixed her father's paints. She painted all over her father's painting. When her father found out, he was furious. Yani cried and cried. She wailed, "But I want to paint like you, Daddy!"

Her father was amazed. He thought of his own childhood. He had also longed to paint. But his parents had been afraid he would make a mess. He decided right then that he would give Yani everything he wished he had as a child.

Yani's father worked with oil paints. But he chose to start Yani in Chinese brush painting. The art of brush painting is very old. Its tools are brushes with bamboo handles, black and colored inks, and thin slips of rice paper. Today Yani is an expert at brush painting.

Getting ready to paint is a process with many steps. First Yani prepares the tools. She sits on the floor. On a low table in front of her are a jug of water, a black grinding stone, hard ink sticks, and brushes in a pottery jar. Then Yani wets the stone with water. Next she rubs the ink stick in slow circles on the stone. She grinds the ink until it is thick and deep black.

Next she takes a piece of rice paper. She places it on the table or, if it's very large, right on the floor. She waits while a picture forms in her head. Then she chooses a brush. She dips it in the freshly ground ink and holds it over the paper. Then she strokes the brush onto the paper. Yani may choose a small or large brush. She can use more or less water. She may make light, watery washes or powerful, thick black marks. She may even flick the brush to spatter the paint. Then the paint looks as if she had rubbed paint-filled brushes over wire screens.

As a very young painter, Yani first made pictures of cats. But soon she switched to monkeys. She had seen monkeys at the zoo. She was enchanted by their playful movements. She wanted to climb into the cage. She stood and watched for hours. She cried when she had to go home. The monkeys filled her thoughts. She began to make up stories about them. Her paintings were a form of storytelling.

Yani loved monkeys so much that her father bought her one for a pet. She named it Lida.

For three years, Yani made monkey paintings. Each one had a bit of the story written beside it. Each one had a wonderful title. "Let Me Smell the Flower" shows a monkey with a bright red blossom in a pottery vase. In "This Is for Mommy," a baby monkey stands on its mother's back. It hands her fruit to eat. "Pull Harder!" shows two groups of monkeys in a tug-of-war.

In some paintings the monkeys act out a scene from Yani's real life. In "I Am Not Scared," a wide-eyed monkey is getting a shot at the doctor's office. Yani painted it when she had to have a shot herself.

When Yani started school, she made new friends. At the same time her paintings began to change. She painted birds and flowers and other new things. Sometimes she painted herself as a monkey and painted her friends as other animals. One painting shows a small monkey holding its arms up between two roosters. It is called "Don't Fight!"

As Yani grew, more and more people
noticed her amazing talent. Her father
introduced her to some painting friends.
Through them she met other artists. Galleries
began to show her work. She began to travel to
other countries where other people discovered
her work.

Yani was born with a great gift. But there are other reasons that she became a skilled and expressive painter. She was raised in a home that loved and encouraged art. Her mother first supported Yani's father, and then Yani herself. Her father has been her guide since she first showed an interest in painting. He did some surprising things to encourage her. In Chinese brush painting, students learn a very exact method. They are expected to hold the brush a certain way. They must copy brushstrokes until they can do them the "right" way.

But Yani's father chose to let her find her own method. He gave her praise. He asked many questions to challenge her. But he never tried to get her to paint his way.

Most amazing of all, her father decided to give up painting himself. He wanted more time to help Yani. He also feared that if he kept painting, Yani might start to paint his way. And he wanted her to develop her own style.

By the time she was a teenager, Yani was a world-famous artist. Her work continues to grow and change. Today she is loved by thousands of people who have come to know her work.